This edition first published in 1993 by
The Promotional Reprint Company Limited,
produced exclusively for Fraser Stewart
Book Wholesale Ltd, Abbey Chambers, 4 Highbridge St
Waltham Abbey, Essex EN9 1DQ

Copyright © Editorial LIBSA, Narciso Serra, 25 – Tel 433 54 07 –
28007 MADRID
4.ª EDICION 1991
Copyright English language text © 1993 Promotional Reprint
Company Limited

ISBN 1 85648 137 9

Printed and bound in China.

SALADS
AND STARTERS

CONTENTS

INTRODUCTION

The range of ingredients which can be used to make a salad is immense, varied and ever increasing. However the worth of most salads lies in the dressing and seasoning. Good quality oil (preferably virgin olive oil) and vinegar are essential in creating a successful salad, whatever other ingredients it might contain. The only other requirement is that the ingredients should always be as fresh as possible.

The term salad is no longer restricted to a simple combination of lettuce, tomato and onion. With time, imagination and, in particular, influences from other countries and cuisines, it has grown to embrace numerous sophisticated combinations of ingredients. Vegetables are no longer the fundamental ingredient; fish, meat, chicken, pulses and fruit have now been added to the list of options, opening up many new and exciting possibilities.

A dish which was previously always served cold, usually in the hot summer months, and often only as an accompaniment, salad has now outgrown these limits and occupies a significant place in every menu, whatever the time of year. Sophisticated salad variations now also include subtle mixtures of cold and warm ingredients – a method initiated by the French school of cooking.

More than any other type of dish, salad allows boundless options for experimentation with different ingredients or absorption of new influences and methods of preparation, and is limited only by the availability of the fresh ingredients.

Hors d'oeuvres follow a slightly more formal pattern, but are still open to imagination. Served as a preliminary to lunch or dinner, hors d'oeuvres, or starters, fulfil the important role of whetting the appetite and stimulating the taste buds, without being too rich or too heavy. Consequently, as in salads, the blends of seasonings and textures are of paramount importance.

GREEN SALADS

SUMMER SALAD

Serves 4

150 ml/5 fl oz olive oil
60 ml/2 fl oz white wine vinegar
salt
2 heads of chicory
1 lettuce
2 cucumbers, sliced
3 carrots, grated

1 red onion, peeled, sliced and pushed out into
* rings*
3 radishes, trimmed and sliced
60 g/2 oz black olives
60 g/2 oz green olives

Mix the olive oil and vinegar and season with salt, to make a vinaigrette.

Wipe the chicory and cut into julienne strips. Wash and dry the lettuce keeping the leaves whole.

Place the lettuce leaves in a bowl. Arrange a ring of cucumber slices on top, then put the chicory and and the grated carrot in the centre. To finish, arrange the onion rings, remaining cucumber slices, radish slices and black olives around the edge of the bowl. Scatter green olives over the carrot and dress with the vinaigrette.

GREEN SALAD WITH WHITE TRUFFLE

Serves 4

1 lettuce heart
12 cooked green asparagus tips
3 celery stalks, chopped
60 g/1 oz white truffles, grated

Dressing:
4 anchovies, soaked in milk and drained
2 hard-boiled eggs, shelled and chopped
150 ml/5 fl oz olive oil
60 ml/2 fl oz white wine vinegar
1 tsp mustard
salt
freshly ground white pepper

Wash and dry the lettuce keeping the leaves whole. Arrange in a bowl and put the cooked asparagus tips in a circle on top. Place the chopped celery in the centre and sprinkle over the grated truffles.

Pound together the anchovies, eggs, oil, mustard and vinegar. Season with salt and pepper and pour over the salad.

WATERCRESS SALAD

Serves 4

150 ml/5 fl oz olive oil
60 ml/2 fl oz white wine vinegar
salt
2 bunches of watercress

Mix the olive oil and vinegar and season with salt to make a vinaigrette.

Wash the watercress thoroughly. Cut into small sprigs, and arrange in a bowl. Pour over the vinaigrette.

Top: Summer Salad
Bottom: Green Salad with White Truffle

ROYAL SALAD

Serves 4

1 curly endive, shredded
1 lettuce, shredded
3 dessert apples, cored and diced
1 small onion, peeled and chopped
2 celery stalks, chopped
2 mint sprigs, finely chopped
seeds of 1 pomegranate
2 tbsp pine nuts
2 tbsp capers
2 hard-boiled eggs, shelled and chopped
1 lemon, thinly sliced

Dressing:
12 anchovies, chopped
3 garlic cloves, chopped
100 g/3½ oz black olives, stoned and chopped
½ tsp cumin
1 tsp oregano
150 ml/5 fl oz olive oil
60 ml/2 fl oz white wine vinegar
pinch sugar
salt

Garnish:
lettuce hearts

Arrange the endive, lettuce, apples, onion and celery on individual plates in circles or squares. Sprinkle over the mint.

Garnish with the pomegranate seeds, pine nuts, capers, egg and lemon slices.

Make the dressing. Mash together the anchovies, garlic, olives, cumin and oregano. Stir in the oil, vinegar and sugar and season with salt. Pour over the salad and garnish with lettuce hearts.

ROMAN SALAD

Serves 4

150 ml/5 fl oz olive oil
60 ml/2 fl oz white wine vinegar
salt
1 lettuce
4 radishes
2 celery stalks
2 radicchio
1 red onion, peeled and finely sliced

Mix together the oil and vinegar and season with salt to make a vinaigrette. Cut the lettuce, radishes, celery stalks and radicchio into coarse julienne strips. Mix together in a bowl with the onion and dress with the vinaigrette.

SPRING SALAD

Serves 4

150 ml/5 fl oz olive oil
60 ml/ 2 fl oz white wine vinegar
salt
1 lettuce
1 bunch spring onions, trimmed
3 tomatoes, sliced

Top: Roman Salad
Bottom: Spring Salad

2 hard-boiled eggs, shelled and quartered
1 bunch radishes, trimmed
100 g/3½ oz black olives

Mix together the oil and vinegar and season with salt to make a vinaigrette.

Wash and dry the lettuce, keeping the leaves whole and arrange in a bowl. Add the spring onions, tomatoes, egg quarters, radishes and olives.

Dress with the vinaigrette.

CURLY ENDIVE, GARLIC AND SHALLOT SALAD

Serves 4

150 ml/5 fl oz olive oil
60 ml/2 fl oz sherry vinegar
salt
1 curly endive
1 garlic clove, crushed
2 shallots, chopped

Mix the oil and vinegar and season with salt to make a vinaigrette.

Wash the endive thoroughly, discarding the greenest leaves and reserving only the most tender ones. Rub the crushed garlic over the inside of a salad bowl. Place the endive leaves and chopped shallots in the bowl and mix together. Dress with the vinaigrette.

MOORISH SALAD

Serves 4

150 ml/5 fl oz olive oil
60 ml/2 fl oz white wine vinegar
salt
1 curly endive
170 g/6 oz olives stuffed with pimientos

2 tsp vegetable oil
100 g/3½ oz bacon, rinds removed and diced

Garnish:
basil leaves

Mix together the olive oil and vinegar and season with salt to make a vinaigrette.

Wash the endive, discarding the darkest leaves and leave it in cold water to soak.

Heat the vegetable oil and fry the bacon.

Below: Moorish Salad
Right: American Salad

Drain and dry the endive and arrange in a bowl with the olives. Pour over the vinaigrette and add the hot bacon just before serving. Garnish with basil leaves.

PRINCE OF WALES SALAD

Serves 4

150 ml/5 fl oz olive oil
60 ml/2 fl oz white wine vinegar
salt
450 g/1 lb fresh anchovies, cleaned
1 curly endive, shredded
1 bunch watercress, chopped
1 tbsp capers
1 tbsp chopped chervil

Mix together the olive oil and vinegar and season with salt to make a vinaigrette.

Blanch the anchovies in boiling, salted water for a few minutes, until just cooked. Allow to cool, bone and cut off the tails.

Place the lettuce and watercress in a bowl. Add the capers and chervil. Dress with the vinaigrette and add the anchovies.

AMERICAN SALAD

Serves 4

90 ml/3 fl oz olive oil
30 ml/1 fl oz white wine vinegar
salt
2 large potatoes
3 celery stalks
1 lettuce

2 large, firm tomatoes, thinly sliced
12 black olives
150-200 ml/5-7 fl oz mayonnaise

Mix together the olive oil and vinegar and season with salt to make a vinaigrette.

Boil the potatoes, drain and set aside to cool. Peel and dice. Cut the celery into julienne strips. Separate the lettuce and tear it into pieces. Place the potatoes, celery and lettuce in a bowl and dress with the vinaigrette. Leave for 30 minutes without mixing.

Arrange the tomatoes and olives around the edge of a serving dish. Mix the potatoes, celery and lettuce well and pile on to the centre of the dish. Serve the mayonnaise separately.

VEGETABLE SALADS

WALDORF SALAD

Serves 4

2 dessert apples, peeled and chopped
1 small head celery, sliced and blanched
2 potatoes, peeled, boiled and diced
3 tbsp mayonnaise
1 lettuce heart
1/2 small can asparagus tips

In a bowl, mix together the apple, celery and potatoes. Stir in the mayonnaise. Using the lettuce leaves as 'boats', fill with the potato mixture. Garnish with the asparagus tips and cherry tomatoes, if liked.

Note: This salad is named after the world-famous New York hotel, the Waldorf Astoria.

RAW ARTICHOKE SALAD

Serves 4

12 globe artichokes
1 hard-boiled egg, shelled
1 tsp mustard
3 tbsp olive oil
1 tbsp white wine vinegar
salt
freshly ground white pepper

Use small, tender artichokes. Prepare them by removing the stalks and the chokes. Arrange the tender leaves in a shallow salad bowl.

Make a dressing by mixing together the yolk of the hard-boiled egg, the mustard, oil, vinegar, pepper and salt.

Pour the dressing over the artichoke leaves. Chop the egg white and use to garnish the salad.

SALADE TIÈDE D'OIGNONS (WARM RED ONION SALAD)

Serves 4

2 red onions
5 tbsp olive oil
2 tbsp red wine vinegar
salt

Preheat the oven to 180°C/350°F, gas mark 4.

Bake the unpeeled onions in the oven for 2 hours.

Remove the onions from the oven, peel and slice. Dress with oil, vinegar and salt and serve immediately.

SPRING GREENS SALAD

Serves 4

150 ml/5 fl oz olive oil
60 ml/2 fl oz white wine vinegar
salt
2 kg/4 1/2 lb spring greens

Mix together the oil and vinegar and season with salt to make a vinaigrette.

Wash the greens thoroughly. Cut off the root, tear off the leaves from the stalk and wash them again. Cook in plenty of boiling, salted water until just tender. Drain well and toss in the vinaigrette. Serve cold.

WHITE CABBAGE SALAD

Serves 4

200 ml/7 fl oz plain yogurt
salt
freshly ground white pepper
450 g/1 lb cabbage, finely shredded
2 carrots, grated
2 apples, peeled, cored and diced
juice of 1/2 lemon
100 g/3 1/2 oz raisins
60 g/2 oz walnuts, chopped
2 tbsp finely chopped onion

Mix together the yogurt, salt and pepper.

In a salad bowl, combine the cabbage, carrots and apples. Pour over the lemon juice and mix again thoroughly.

Add the raisins, walnuts and onion and stir in the yogurt.

SALAD OF CRUDITÉS

Serves 4

2 lettuce hearts
2 celery stalks
1 cucumber
2 radishes
2 carrots
2 heads chicory
5 tbsp olive oil
2 tbsp white wine vinegar
salt

Separate the lettuce leaves. Cut the celery, cucumber, radishes, carrots and chicory lengthwise into fine strips. Arrange the lettuce on a serving plate set over a salad bowl filled with ice. Arrange the the vegetables on top. Serve accompanied by a vinaigrette dressing.

RUSSIAN SALAD

Serves 6

1kg/2 1/4 lb potatoes
250 g/9 oz carrots, diced
250 g/9 oz French beans, sliced
250 g/9 oz shelled peas
250 g/9 oz cooked beetroot, diced
300 ml/10 fl oz mayonnaise
1 tsp capers
1 head chicory, sliced

Cook the unpeeled potatoes in lightly salted boiling water for about 20 minutes, until tender. Drain, set aside to cool and cut into cubes.

Simmer the carrots, beans and peas together until just tender. Drain and cool.

Place all the vegetables in a bowl and mix in the mayonnaise. Sprinkle over the capers.

Top: Waldorf Salad
Bottom: Russian Salad

ITALIAN SALAD OF ARTICHOKE HEARTS

Serves 6

12 artichokes
5 tbsp olive oil
2 tbsp white wine vinegar
salt
1/2 tsp mustard
6 radishes, sliced

If you are using fresh artichokes, simmer them until tender. Drain and remove the chokes. Cut the artichoke hearts into chunks and arrange in 1 large serving or 6 individual bowls.

Mix together the oil, vinegar, and mustard and season with salt to make a vinaigrette dressing.

Pour the vinaigrette over the artichoke hearts and serve them garnished with the radish slices.

ASPARAGUS SALAD

Serves 4

500 g/1 lb 2 oz lb asparagus
200 g/7 oz mixed lettuce leaves
1 avocado pear
few drops of lemon juice
150 g/5 oz button mushrooms, sliced

Dressing:
5 tbsp extra virgin olive oil
2 tbsp sherry vinegar
salt
freshly ground black pepper

Boil the asparagus until it is tender. Drain. Wash the lettuce leaves and pat dry.

Cut the avocado pear into small pieces and sprinkle with lemon juice.

Mix the salad ingredients together in a bowl. Add the dressing and the asparagus just before serving. Stir again and serve.

MYKONOS SALAD

Serves 4

4 aubergines
2 tomatoes, chopped
1 small onion, peeled and chopped
2 garlic cloves, chopped
5 tbsp olive oil
2 tbsp white wine vinegar
salt
freshly ground black pepper
2 green peppers, seeded and sliced in rings
60 g/2 oz black olives

Preheat the oven to 180° C/350° F, gas mark 4.

Wash and dry the aubergines and bake in the oven for 1 1/2 hours until the skin turns brown. Peel and cut them into large pieces, discarding the seeds. Mix together all the ingredients, except the peppers and olives, and dress with oil, vinegar, salt and pepper. Serve in a shallow earthenware dish, garnished with green pepper rings and olives.

CARROT AND RAISIN SALAD

Serves 4

juice of 1 orange
juice of 1 lemon
5 tbsp olive oil
1/2 tsp white wine vinegar
salt
freshly ground black pepper
100 g/3 1/2 oz raisins
5 carrots
2 heads chicory

Left top: Italian Salad of Artichoke Hearts
Left bottom: Asparagus Salad
Right top: Mykonos Salad
Right bottom: Carrot and Raisin Salad

First, make the dressing. Combine the fruit juices with the oil and vinegar. Season with salt and pepper to taste. Add the raisins and allow to stand for 2 hours.

Wash and grate the carrots and cut the chicory lengthwise. Place on a serving dish and pour over the dressing.

GREEN AND WHITE ASPARAGUS SALAD

Serves 6

12 white asparagus spears
12 green asparagus spears
5 tbsp olive oil
2 tbsp white wine vinegar
salt
3 hard-boiled eggs, shelled and chopped
1 tomato, finely diced

Boil the green and white asparagus separately. Drain and set aside.

Combine the oil and vinegar and season with salt to make a vinaigrette.

Arrange the asparagus in alternate colours on a serving dish. Pour over a little vinaigrette, reserving the rest.

Sprinkle some of the chopped eggs and tomatoes over the asparagus. Mix the remainder with the reserved vinaigrette and serve separately.

CELERY HEART SALAD

Serves 4

1 head celery
4 tbsp mayonnaise

Lightly cook the celery in boiling, salted water. Allow to cool, then cut off the top part. Slice the rest into small pieces and mix in the mayonnaise. Serve cold, garnished with colourful vegetables, if liked.

Right: Green and White Asparagus Salad
Far right: Celery Heart Salad

CELERY AND COTTAGE CHEESE SALAD

Serves 4

500 g/1 lb 2 oz cottage cheese
3 celery stalks, finely chopped
1 lettuce heart, finely shredded
salt
freshly ground black pepper
100 g/3½ oz walnuts, chopped
60 g/2 oz currants

Mix together the cottage cheese, celery and lettuce. Season with salt and pepper to taste. Divide among individual bowls and sprinkle with the chopped walnuts and currants and serve.

GREEN CABBAGE SALAD

Serves 4

1 green cabbage
2 carrots
1 onion
2 tbsp white wine vinegar
1 tsp mustard
5 tbsp olive oil
salt

Shred the cabbage finely and soak in cold water for 30 minutes.

Drain the cabbage well. Cut the carrots and the onion into julienne strips. Mix with the cabbage.

Make a vinaigrette. Mix together the vinegar and the mustard. Add the oil, a little at a time, whisking continuously. Season to taste.

Pour the dressing over the salad and chill in the refrigerator for 30 minutes before serving.

CELERY AND RAISIN SALAD

Serves 4

100 g/3½ oz raisins
juice of 1 lemon
grated rind and juice of 1 orange
1 head celery, chopped
5 walnuts, finely chopped
1 tomato, chopped
1 apple, chopped
7 fl oz olive oil
salt
freshly ground black pepper

Marinate the raisins in the fruit juices for 30 minutes.

Place the celery, walnuts, tomato and apple in a serving bowl. Add the raisins and marinade. Drizzle over the oil and sprinkle with a little grated orange rind. Season to taste.

RACHEL SALAD

Serves 4

4 potatoes
1 medium can artichoke hearts
½ head celery
1 truffle, finely sliced
5 fl oz olive oil
2 fl oz white wine vinegar
salt
1 small can asparagus tips

Cook, peel and dice the potatoes. Cut the artichokes into pieces of equal size. Wash and boil the celery and cut into strips. Finely slice the truffle.

Place all the ingredients in a bowl, dress with the oil, vinegar and salt and decorate with the asparagus tips.

An alternative dressing for this salad is mayonnaise. In this case, omit the truffle.

Top: Celery and Cottage Cheese Salad
Bottom: Celery and Raisin Salad

WHITE CABBAGE, PEANUT AND RAISIN SALAD

Serves 4

1 white cabbage, finely sliced
4 apples, finely chopped
60 g/2 oz raisins
60 g/2 oz roasted peanuts, finely chopped
10 fl oz mayonnaise
2 tbsp chopped parsley
salt
freshly ground black pepper

Combine all the salad ingredients in bowl, stir in the mayonnaise and season with salt and pepper.

Chill in the refrigerator for at least 30 minutes before serving.

INSALATA ZUCCHINI (ITALIAN COLD COURGETTE SALAD)

Serves 4

2 courgettes, trimmed and sliced
2 tbsp olive oil
2 tsp white wine vinegar
salt

Cook the courgettes in boiling, salted water until *al dente*, that is, tender but still firm to the bite.

Set aside to cool. Dress with the oil and vinegar and season with salt.

Alternatively, sprinkle with vinegar and aromatic herbs.

BEETROOT SALAD

Serves 4

4 fresh beetroot
1 hard-boiled egg, shelled and chopped
salt
2 tbsp olive oil
2 tsp vinegar

Cook the beetroot until tender and set aside to cool.

Peel and slice the beetroot. Arrange it on a serving dish and pile the chopped egg in the centre. Season with salt and add the oil and vinegar.

PEPPER AND POTATO SALAD

Serves 4

1 kg/2¼ lb potatoes
salt
4 red peppers
2 hard-boiled eggs, shelled
5 tbsp virgin olive oil
2 tbsp sherry vinegar

Cook the potatoes in their skins in plenty of lightly salted boiling water. Drain and set aside to cool.

When the potatoes are cool, peel and cut them into slices.

Grill or roast the peppers in the oven at 200° C/4000° F, gas mark 6 until the skins are black and blistered. Allow to cool so that they can be handled. Peel and seed the peppers and cut them into strips.

Sieve the yolk and finely chop the white of the eggs. Arrange the potatoes and peppers in a bowl and sprinkle over the egg white and yolk. Dress with virgin olive oil, sherry vinegar and season with salt to taste.

PIPIRRANA SALAD

Serves 4

3 red peppers
2 onions, peeled and finely chopped
3 tomatoes, skinned, seeded and finely chopped

Top: Beetroot Salad
Bottom: Insalata Zucchini (Italian Cold Courgette Salad)

5 tbsp olive oil
2 tbsp white wine vinegar
salt
1 garlic clove, finely chopped
200 g/7 oz canned tuna
2 hard-boiled eggs, shelled and finely chopped

Grill or roast the peppers at 200° C/400° F, gas mark 6 until the skins are black and blistered. Allow to cool so that you can handle them, then peel, seed and cut them into strips.

Mix together the peppers, onions and tomatoes in an earthenware bowl. Add the oil, vinegar, salt and garlic.

Add the tuna and chopped egg, mix well and chill in the refrigerator before serving.

BASIL SALAD

Serves 4

4 small courgettes, finely sliced
3 tbsp finely chopped basil
juice of 1/2 lemon
salt
freshly ground black pepper

Arrange the courgettes in a salad bowl. Scatter over the basil, dress with the lemon juice, and season with salt and pepper.

MUSHROOM AND CUCUMBER SALAD

Serves 4

120 ml/4 fl oz olive oil
30 ml/1 fl oz white wine vinegar
1 bay leaf, crumbled
1 rosemary sprig
1 tarragon sprig
salt
freshly ground black pepper
120 g/4 oz mushrooms, sliced
1/2 cucumber, thickly sliced
350 g/12 oz tomatoes, sliced
1 lettuce

Mix together the oil, vinegar, herbs and salt and pepper to taste. Put the mushrooms and cucumber in a bowl and pour over the dressing. Set aside to marinate for 30 minutes.

Arrange the lettuce leaves in a salad bowl. Drain the mushrooms and cucumber and arrange on top. Garnish with the tomato slices. Strain the dressing and pour over the salad just before serving.

Pipirrana Salad

RICE, PULSE AND PASTA SALADS

RICE SALAD

Serves 6

400 g/14 oz rice
salt
1 x 200 g/7 oz can tuna, drained and flaked
1 tbsp Worcestershire sauce
1 tbsp finely chopped onion
2 tbsp olive oil
1 tbsp finely chopped parsley
juice of 1 lemon
2 tomatoes, thinly sliced
1 hard-boiled egg, shelled and thinly sliced
150 g/5 oz cooked peas
1 fresh or canned pepper (pimiento)
60 g/2 oz black olives
60 g/2 oz capers
90 g/3 oz Gruyère cheese, cheese

Cook the rice in lightly salted boiling water for 20 minutes. Drain, rinse under cold running water and place on a serving dish.

Mix together the tuna, Worcestershire sauce, onion, oil, parsley and lemon juice and season with salt. Reserve a little of the mixture and incorporate the remainder in the rice, mixing well.

Garnish the rice with alternate slices of tomato and egg, sprinkle over the peas and arrange strips of pepper all around the dish. Pour over the remaining dressing, place the olives and capers in the centre and sprinkle the grated Gruyère cheese on top.

FETTUCCINE AND SARDINE SALAD

Serves 6

500 g/1 lb 2 oz fettuccine
salt
2 cans sardines in oil
2 hard-boiled egg yolks, sieved
6 canned pimientos, finely chopped
100 g/3½ oz black olives, stoned
2 tbsp olive oil

Cook the fettuccine in plenty of lightly salted boiling water for 8-10 minutes, until *al dente*, that is just tender but still firm to the bite. Rinse thoroughly under cold running water, drain well and place in a serving dish.

Meanwhile, mash the sardines with a fork, discarding the backbones. Add the egg yolks, pimientos and olives. Stir in the oil and mix well. Add the mixture to the fettuccine, mix well and serve.

CHICKPEA SALAD

Serves 6

500 g/1 lb 2 oz chickpeas, soaked overnight
  and drained
10 fl oz olive oil
4 tbsp white wine vinegar
salt
4 tomatoes, skinned, seeded and finely chopped
1 large onion, peeled and finely chopped
1 medium can tuna (optional)
2 hard-boiled eggs, shelled and chopped
  (optional)

Cook the chickpeas in plenty of boiling, unsalted water for at least 1½ hours until very tender. (Once dressed with the vinaigrette, they will harden.)

Drain the chickpeas and reserve some of the cooking liquid. Set the chickpeas aside to cool.

Make a vinaigrette by beating together the oil, vinegar and salt with a little of the reserved cooking liquid.

Place the chickpeas in a salad bowl, add the tomatoes and onion, pour over the dressing and mix thoroughly. Add the tuna and chopped hard-boiled egg, if using.

Note: This dish is equally tasty if you crush a couple of cloves of garlic and 1 tsp cumin seeds, into the vinaigrette.

PASTA SHELLS AND ASPARAGUS

Serves 6

500 g/1 lb 2 oz pasta shells
salt
225 g/8 oz asparagus
2 tbsp single cream
2 tbsp mayonnaise

Cook the pasta shells in lightly salted boiling water for 8-10 minutes, until *al dente*, that is, just tender but still firm to the bite.

Drain and cool under cold running water. Set aside.

Loosely tie the asparagus together and cook upright in lightly salted boiling water. Drain and reserve only the tender top parts. Cut into pieces.

Mix the pasta shells together with the asparagus. Stir the cream into the mayonnaise and toss with the pasta and asparagus. Serve cold.

RICE AND RAISIN SALAD

Serves 4

30 g/1 oz raisins
100 g/3½ oz rice
salt
½ cold roast chicken, boned and chopped
2 tomatoes, sliced
1 red pepper, seeded and sliced
3 carrots, finely diced
100 g/3½ oz black olives, stoned and finely
  chopped
60 ml/2 fl oz grapeseed oil
2 tsp white wine vinegar

Soak the raisins in warm water .

Boil the rice in plenty of lightly salted water for 15 minutes. Drain and rinse in cold water, so that the grains are separated.

Place the rice on a serving dish. Add the chicken, tomatoes, pepper and carrots. Sprinkle over the raisins and olives. Dress with the oil and the vinegar and season with salt.

RICE AND ONION SALAD

Serves 4

100 g/3½ oz rice
salt
1 tbsp sunflower oil
1 tbsp clear honey
2 tbsp white wine vinegar
freshly ground black pepper
120 g/4 oz mushrooms, sliced
120 g/4 oz French beans, cooked, drained,
  cooled and diced
350 g/12 oz tomatoes, sliced
1 bunch spring onions, trimmed and chopped
½ bunch radishes, trimmed and sliced
1 lettuce

Top: Rice Salad
Bottom: Rice and Raisin Salad

Cook the rice in lightly salted boiling water for 20 minutes. Drain and rinse under cold running water.

Beat together the oil, honey and wine vinegar and season to taste. Pour the dressing over the rice and toss lightly.

Mix together the rice, mushrooms, beans, tomatoes, spring onions and radishes.

Line a salad bowl with lettuce leaves and pile the rice mixture on top. Serve cold.

Note: 60 g/2 oz salted roast peanuts may be added to this salad to provide an additional crunchy texture.

SPAGHETTI AND ANCHOVY SALAD

Serves 4

500 g/1 lb 2 oz spaghetti
salt
1 can anchovies, drained and chopped, oil reserved
2 ripe tomatoes, skinned, seeded and sieved
2 firm tomatoes, skinned, seeded and chopped
2 tbsp capers
100 g/3½ oz olives

Cook the spaghetti in plenty of lightly salted boilingwater. Rinse under cold running water, drain and reserve.

Add the oil from the anchovies to the sieved tomato and mix. Pour this sauce over the spaghetti and mix well with a wooden spoon. Chill in the refrigerator for 30 minutes.

Just before serving, stir in the anchovies, chopped tomatoes, capers and olives.

SEAFOOD AND RICE SALAD

Serves 4

1.5 kg/3¼ lb mixed mussels and clams
60 ml/2 fl oz dry white wine
400 g/14 oz rice
100 g/3½ oz fresh prawns, peeled and deveined
100 g/3½ oz button mushrooms, fresh or canned, finely sliced
1 tbsp chopped parsley
salt
freshly ground black pepper

Dressing:
2 hard-boiled eggs, shelled
6 saffron threads
1 tbsp olive oil
dash Worcestershire sauce
salt
freshly ground black pepper

Scrub the mussels and clams under cold running water, discarding any which do not shut when sharply tapped. Heat them in a large pan with the wine, discarding any which do not open. Strain and remove and discard the shells.

Cook the rice in boiling, salted water, drain and allow to cool. Place on a serving dish and mix in the shellfish and mushrooms. To make the dressing, mash the eggs in a bowl, gradually add the oil, saffron and Worcestershire sauce and season with salt and pepper. Pour over the salad, mix and sprinkle over the chopped parsley.

SAUSAGE AND PASTA SPIRAL SALAD

Serves 6

500 g/1 lb 2 oz pasta spirals
100 ml/3½ fl oz cream
60 ml/2 fl oz milk
juice of ½ lemon
100 ml/3½ fl oz thick mayonnaise
300 g/10 oz German cured sausages, sliced
6 gherkins, sliced

Left: Seafood and Rice Salad
Top Right: Spaghetti and Anchovy Salad
Bottom Right: Sausage and Pasta Spiral Salad

Cook the pasta until 'al dente'. Drain and allow to cool. Mix the cream, milk and lemon juice into the mayonnaise. Place the pasta in a serving dish. Stir in the sausages, gherkins and dressing. Serve immediately.

CHICKPEA AND PEPPER SALAD

Serves 6

450 g/1 lb chickpeas, soaked overnight
6 canned pimentos, chopped
3 green peppers, diced
2 celery stalks, chopped
150 ml/5 fl oz mayonnaise

Simmer the chickpeas until tender. Alternatively, use drained, canned chickpeas.

In a serving dish, arrange the chickpeas, pimentos, green peppers and celery.

Two hours before serving, mix the mayonnaise into the salad.

TUNA AND HARICOT BEAN SALAD

Serves 6

1 kg/2¼ lb haricot beans
1 large can tuna
juice of ½ lemon
5 tbsp olive oil

freshly ground white pepper
1 onion, peeled and sliced

Simmer the beans, with a little oil, until tender. Drain and allow to cool. Place in a serving dish, mix in the tuna and dress with a mixture of lemon juice, oil and pepper. Garnish with onion slices and tomato, if liked.

LENTIL SALAD

Serves 6

500 g/1 lb 2 oz lentils
2 onions, peeled
1 bayleaf
5 tbsp olive oil
2 tbsp white wine vinegar
1 tsp grain mustard
freshly ground white pepper
4 tomatoes, skinned, seeded and finely chopped
1 tbsp chopped parsley

Wash the lentils, cover with cold water and soak for at least 6 hours. Drain, place in a saucepan and cover with cold water. Add one onion and the bayleaf, and bring to the boil. Lower the heat, then simmer for about 1½ hours, depending on the type of lentil.

Strain, discard the onion and the bayleaf and turn into a serving dish.

Finely chop the remaining onion. Prepare a vinaigrette with the olive oil, vinegar, mustard and pepper. Add the chopped tomato, onion and a little chopped parsley to the lentils and dress with the vinaigrette. Mix well and chill for 2-3 hours. Sprinkle with the remaining parsley just before serving.

Left: Chickpea and Pepper Salad
Right: Tuna and Haricot Bean Salad

FISH AND SHELLFISH

COD SALAD

Serves 4

2 x 200 g/7 oz cooked cod fillets
4 tbsp mayonnaise
2 tbsp capers

Flake the fish. Arrange in a serving dish, add the mayonnaise and sprinkle with the capers.

PRAWN AND WILD MUSHROOM SALAD

Serves 6

1 curly endive, chopped
3 heads chicory, chopped
3 tomatoes, skinned, seeded and diced
salt
150 ml/5 fl oz virgin olive oil
few drops of sherry vinegar
1 kg/2¼ lb cooked prawns
1 kg/2¼ lb wild (or button) mushrooms, trimmed
1 garlic clove, peeled and crushed
chopped parsley
juice of ½ a lemon

Arrange the endive, chicory and tomatoes in a salad bowl and season with salt. Dress with the oil and sherry vinegar. Reserve. Peel the prawns and cut each one in half lengthways. Sauté the mushrooms in a frying-pan in a little oil and the garlic, then stir in the chopped parsley. Sauté the prawns separately and add a little lemon juice at the end.

Using the salad as a base, arrange the prawns on one side and the mushrooms on the other. Serve warm.

PIKE SALAD

Serves 6

bouquet garni
150 ml/5 fl oz olive oil
60 ml/2 fl oz white wine vinegar
1 x 800 g/1¾ lb pike
1 garlic clove, peeled and crushed
2 tbsp chopped parsley
2 pickled peppers, sliced
6 anchovies, soaked in milk
2 tsp capers

Bring a large pan of salted water to the boil. Add the bouquet garni and 1 teaspoon of the olive oil, then add the pike. Cover and simmer for about 35 minutes, until just cooked. Drain, allow to cool, then skin and bone. Cut into bite-sized pieces and reserve.

Pound the garlic in a mortar with the parsley and mix well with the oil and vinegar. Arrange the pike pieces on a serving dish, garnish with the strips of pepper, anchovies and capers, and dress with the garlic sauce.

TURIN SALAD

Serves 4

700 g/1½ lb button mushrooms, finely sliced
60 g/2 oz parsley, chopped
6 anchovy fillets, soaked and chopped
2 egg yolks, beaten
1 garlic clove
squeeze of lemon juice

Arrange the mushrooms in a salad bowl. In another bowl, put the parsley, anchovies and egg yolks. Spear the garlic clove with a fork and stir the mixture, in one direction only, until it becomes creamy. Stir in the lemon juice, pour over the mushrooms and serve.

LA SCALA ANCHOVY SALAD

Serves 4

450 g/1 lb French beans
1 small can anchovies, drained and chopped
1 medium can pimentos, drained and chopped
2 hard-boiled eggs, shelled and chopped
5 fl oz olive oil
2 fl oz white wine vinegar
salt
1 tbsp chopped parsley

Cook the beans in salted, boiling water until just tender.

In a salad bowl, mix the beans, anchovies, pimentos and eggs. Make a vinaigrette with the olive oil and vinegar, season with salt, and use to dress the salad. Sprinkle with chopped parsley.

GRANADA MARINADE

Serves 6

550 g/1¼ lb salt cod, soaked overnight
6 oranges, peeled and chopped
60 g/2 oz pitted olives
6 spring onions, chopped
4 tbsp oil
1 tbsp sherry vinegar
1 tsp paprika
1 garlic clove, crushed
salt
3 hard-boiled eggs, shelled and finely chopped

Bake the cod in a preheated oven at 180°C/350°F, gas mark 4 for about 30 minutes until lightly browned. Allow to cool, skin and flake the flesh.

Combine the oranges, olives and spring onions. Dress with oil, vinegar, paprika, garlic and salt. Mix in the fish and enough cold water to moisten. Stir in the chopped eggs and chill before serving.

Top: Cod Salad
Bottom: Turin Salad

CRAYFISH SALAD

Serves 4

1 bayleaf
1 kg/2¼ lb fresh crayfish
1 lettuce, shredded
150 ml/5 fl oz olive oil
20 ml/2 fl oz white wine vinegar
salt
1 hard-boiled egg, shelled and chopped
  (optional)
1 small onion, peeled and finely chopped
1 small gherkin, finely chopped

Bring a large pan of water to the boil, add the bayleaf and crayfish and cook for 3 minutes. Remove, drain and allow to cool, discarding the bayleaf. Separate the tail meat from the heads. Arrange the lettuce on a serving dish. Top with the crayfish with the heads pointing outwards and the tails inwards.

Make a vinaigrette with the olive oil and vinegar and season with salt. Mix in the chopped, hard-boiled egg, onion and gherkins, if using. Use to dress the crayfish tails

DUBLIN BAY PRAWNS AND SPINACH SALAD

Serves 6

250 g/9 oz spinach, briefly cooked
90 ml/3 fl oz olive oil
salt
pepper
3 spring onions
24 Dublin Bay prawns
225 ml/8 fl oz sparkling wine

Arrange the spinach leaves on 6 small plates, dress each with a little olive oil, salt and pepper.

Cut the spring onions into julienne strips and soften them in a large frying pan in a little oil. Add the prawns and sauté for about 20 minutes until cooked through. Add most of the wine 3 minutes before the end.

Remove the prawns from the pan, reserve the heads, clean the tails and keep warm. Return the heads to the pan, add the remaining wine and reduce the sauce.

Arrange the prawns on each bed of spinach and pour over the reduced sauce.

Far Left: Crayfish Salad
Left Dublin Bay Prawns and Spinach Salad

SMOKED SALMON AND WHITEBAIT SALAD

Serves 6

500 g/1 lb 2 oz cooked whitebait
300 g/10 oz smoked salmon, finely sliced
3 fl oz olive oil
juice of ¹/₂ a lemon
salt
2 heads chicory, finely sliced
2 tbsp chopped fresh herbs, e.g. thyme, coriander

The traditional Spanish recipe uses elvers (baby eels) instead of whitebait.

Arrange the whitebait and smoked salmon in a salad bowl. Dress with oil and the lemon juice. Season with salt.

Surround with the sliced chicory and garnish with fresh herbs.

COCKLE SALAD

Serves 6

2 kg/4¹/₂ lb cockles

2 tbsp chopped parsley
5 fl oz olive oil
2 fl oz white wine vinegar
salt

Scrub the cockles under cold running water and discard any which do not close when sharply tapped. Steam in a large saucepan, discarding any which do not open. Remove and discard the shells. Arrange the cockles on a large serving dish. Prepare a vinaigrette with the parsley, oil, vinegar and salt. Pour over the cockles and allow to marinate for at least 1 hour. Serve cold.

ELVER SALAD

Serves 6

550 g/1¹/₄ lb cooked elvers
2 tbsp olive oil
squeeze of lemon juice
1 onion, peeled and chopped
2 garlic cloves, chopped
1 tbsp chopped parsley

Place the elvers in a bowl. Stir in the oil, lemon juice, onion and garlic, leave to rest for a few minutes.

Serve heaped on individual plates, garnished with parsley.

Alternatively, substitute whitebait for the elvers.

SMOKED SALMON SALAD

Serves 4

300 g/10 oz smoked salmon
1 lettuce heart
2 tbsp olive oil

Cut the salmon into medium size strips. Arrange the lettuce leaves on a serving dish and top with the salmon. Pour on the olive oil.

Top: Smoked Salmon and Whitebait Salad
Bottom: Elver Salad

MEAT SALADS

VERONESE CHICKEN SALAD

Serves 6

1 chicken
pinch salt
1 tsp vegetable oil
1 celery stalk
100 g/3¹/₂ oz Emmenthal cheese, chopped
300 ml/10 fl oz mayonnaise

Simmer the chicken, with the salt and oil, for about 1¹/₄ hours or until tender, depending on size. Drain, cool, skin, bone and cut into small pieces. Reserve. Cut the celery into julienne strips.

Mix the chicken and celery with the mayonnaise, which should not be too thick. Serve cold in a salad bowl.

CALVES' MUZZLE SALAD

Serves 6

1 kg/2¹/₄ lb calves' muzzle
salt
saltpetre
sugar (twice the weight of the saltpetre)
few sprigs parsley
freshly ground black pepper
1 clove
2 onions, peeled and sliced
200 g/7 oz gherkins, sliced
300 ml/10 fl oz mayonnaise

This is a traditional recipe from Spain, where veal snout is a much prized meat. A suitably-sized York ham would make a good substitute.

Soak the calves' muzzle in a vinegar and water solution for 1 hour. Season with salt, add saltpetre and soak for a further 48 hours.

Rinse thoroughly under the cold tap. Place in a flameproof casserole, add enough water to cover, and some parsley, black pepper and the clove.
Simmer until cooked, drain, allow to cool and cut into small pieces or fillets.

Arrange the meat, onions and gherkins in a salad bowl. Add enough mayonnaise

to mix well. Serve cold.

SPRAT SALAD

Serves 4

1 kg/2¹/₄ lb small sprats

120 ml/4 fl oz olive oil
juice of 1 lemon
2 tbsp finely chopped parsley

Cook the sprats in boiling water for less than 1 minute. Allow to cool and dress with the oil, lemon juice and parsley.

Top: Calves' Muzzle Salad
Bottom: Veronese Chicken Salad

SADDLE OF HARE SALAD

Serves 6

2 tbsp vegetable oil
1 x 1 kg/2¼ lb saddle of hare
100 ml/3½ fl oz full-bodied red wine
100 ml/3½ fl oz meat stock
60 g/2 oz candied orange peel, chopped
2 tbsp raisins
2 tbsp pine nuts
2 heaped tbsp capers
3 tbsp cooked redcurrants
1 celery stalk, cut into julienne strips

This is a recipe of Bartholomew Stefani's, chef at the court of the Gonzagas.

Heat the oil in a frying-pan and sauté the saddle pieces slowly for 30-40 minutes. Towards the end of cooking time, add the wine and meat stock and simmer to reduce. Allow to cool.

Arrange on the cooked, cooled hare joints on a serving dish and sprinkle with the chopped orange peel, raisins, pine nuts, capers, redcurrants, and celery. Dress with the reduced sauce.

SMOKED DUCK SALAD

Serves 6

550 g/1¼ lb smoked duck, finely sliced
6 radishes
200 g/7 oz corn salad
1 box mustard and cress, snipped
150 ml/5 fl oz olive oil
60 ml/2 fl oz white wine vinegar
salt

Smoked duck is available from most good delicatessens. Cut the radishes to form flowers.

Arrange the duck slices on each plate in the shape of a fan. Garnish with the vegetables. Make a vinaigrette with the oil and vinegar and season with the salt. Use to dress the duck and salad vegetables.

QUAIL SALAD

Serves 6

4 tbsp vegetable oil
3 tbsp white wine vinegar
2 onions, peeled and chopped
2 garlic cloves, crushed
2 carrots, diced
5 black peppercorns
1 bayleaf
6 quails, jointed
5 tbsp olive oil
salt

Heat the oil in a frying-pan and lightly fry the onion, garlic, carrots, peppercorns and bayleaf. Add the quails in two layers, the breasts on top of the legs. Fry until lightly coloured, then add enough water just to cover the vegetables, and 1 tbsp of the vinegar. Cover and simmer for about 30 minutes.

When cooked, remove and bone only the breasts. Arrange all the meat on a bed of lettuce in a serving dish. Purée the carrot and onion mixture in a liquidizer. Mix together the olive oil and remaining vinegar and season with salt. Stir 2 tbsp of the carrot and onion mixture into the vinaigrette, pour over the quail and serve warm.

MUNICH SALAD

Serves 6

6 apples
juice of 1 lemon
700 g/1½ lb potatoes
1 bayleaf
450 g/1 lb Frankfurters, thinly sliced
300 g/10 oz cured German sausages, thinly sliced
1 medium jar gherkins, thinly sliced
2 onions, peeled and finely sliced
300 ml/10 fl oz mayonnaise

Dice the apples, and toss in lemon juice to prevent discoloration. Reserve. Boil the potatoes in plenty of water with the bayleaf. Peel and dice when cool.

Place all the ingredients in a serving dish, add the mayonnaise and mix well. Serve cold.

Top: Saddle of Hare Salad
Bottom: Smoked Duck Salad

TROPICAL SALADS

DUBLIN BAY PRAWN AND MELON SALAD

Serves 6

1 melon
12 cooked Dublin Bay prawns, shelled
1 tbsp olive oil
4 tbsp mayonnaise
juice of ¹/₂ lemon
4 tbsp single cream
1 tsp curry powder
salt
1 tbsp chopped parsley
6 vine leaves, washed

Cut the melon in half, discard the seeds and scoop out the flesh with a melon baller. Reserve.

Sauté the prawns in the oil over a gentle heat.

In a bowl, mix together the mayonnaise, lemon juice, cream, curry powder and a little salt, if desired.

Arrange the vine leaves on a serving dish. Place the melon balls and the prawns on top. Dress with the sauce and sprinkle with parsley.

TROPICAL SALAD

Serves 4

1 lettuce
100 g/3¹/₂ oz strawberries
1 apple, sliced
100 g/3¹/₂ oz walnuts
100 g/3¹/₂ oz stoned prunes, chopped
60 g/2 oz desiccated coconut
few celery leaves
1 tbsp lemon juice
150 ml/5 fl oz mayonnaise

Arrange a bed of lettuce in a serving dish. Arrange all the ingredients on top, except the lemon juice and mayonnaise. Chill. Stir the lemon juice into the mayonnaise and serve separately.

AVOCADO WITH OYSTERS

Serves 4

2 ripe avocados
12 oysters
2 hard-boiled eggs, yolks only, sieved

3 tbsp olive oil
juice of ¹/₂ lemon
salt

pepper

Cut the avocados in half and remove the

Left: Caribbean Salad
Right: Tropical Salad

stones and flesh, reserving the shells. Dice the flesh and return to the shells. Open the oysters and place 3, together with their juices, into each avocado shell. Mix together the egg yolks, oil, and lemon juice and season with salt and pepper. Once thickened, pour over the avocados.

CARIBBEAN SALAD

Serves 4

200 g/7 oz fresh pineapple
2 tomatoes, finely sliced
1 lettuce
200 g/7 oz sweetcorn
4 tbsp mayonnaise
2 tsp tomato purée
sprig parsley

Peel the pineapple carefully, slice and then cut into evenly sized pieces, discarding the hard core but reserving the green top. Arrange all the ingredients, except the mayonnaise and tomato purée, on a serving dish, using the pineapple top as a decoration. Blend together the mayonnaise and tomato purée and use to dress the salad. Garnish with the parsley sprig.

FRUIT SALADS

PINEAPPLE, ORANGE AND SWEETCORN SALAD

Serves 6

2 corn on the cob, cooked
4 oranges
1 ripe pineapple

Remove the corn from the cob. Peel the oranges, divide into segments and cut in half. Peel the pineapple, quarter lengthways, remove the core and discard, and slice the fruit into triangles. Mix together all the ingredients and serve.

PAGODA FRUIT SALAD

Serves 6

3 mangoes
3 guavas
3 papayas
5 lychees
juice of 3 oranges
juice of 1 lemon
100 ml/3½ fl oz saki
3 kiwi fruit

Wash thoroughly and dry all the fruit. Peel the mangoes, guavas and papayas. Cut the flesh into thick slices and reserve the peel.

Peel and stone the lychees. Purée in a liquidizer, half the flesh with the reserved peel from the other fruit. Strain and add the orange and lemon juice. Mix well and add the saki. Peel and slice the kiwi fruit.

Arrange the fruit on a dish. Garnish with kiwi fruit and the remaining lychees. Pour over the juices and allow to marinate in the refrigerator for 1 hour before serving.

GRAPE SALAD

Serves 6

2 bunches black grapes
2 bunches white grapes
3 bunches muscat grapes
4 tbsp raisins
4 tbsp currants
60 g/2 oz walnuts, chopped

Wash and seed the grapes. Reserve one third of the muscat grapes and place the remainder in a bowl. Purée the reserved grapes in a liquidizer, strain and chill.

Add the raisins and currants to the grapes, pour over the chilled juice, sprinkle with the walnuts and serve.

FOREST BERRY SALAD

Serves 6

250 g/9 oz blackberries
250 g/9 oz redcurrants
250 g/9 oz raspberries
90 g/3 oz sugar
350 ml/12 fl oz water
sprig of mint

Wash the berries and allow to drain thoroughly. Arrange them attractively in a serving dish or individual bowls.

Prepare a light syrup. Put the sugar and water into a heavy based saucepan. Bring to the boil slowly, stirring occasionally, and boil for 5 minutes. Allow to cool slightly. Chop the mint finely and stir into the syrup. Allow to stand for 2 hours then pour over the fruit. Serve, on a bed of fresh vine leaves, if liked.

CHEESE AND FRUIT SALAD

Serves 4

1 orange
2 apples
2 mandarines
300 g/10 oz Mozzarella cheese
150 ml/5 fl oz yoghurt

Peel and dice the fruit. Cut the cheese into fairly large, but thin, triangles. Mix the fruit and yoghurt and arrange on the cheese slices, serving as individual portions.

APPLE AND DATE SALAD

Serves 4

1 lettuce heart, chopped
1 head celery
4 apples, peeled, coved and diced
150 g/5 oz dates, stoned and sliced
2 tbsp chopped mint
300 ml/10 fl oz yoghurt
150 g/5 oz roasted pistachio nuts, chopped

Place the lettuce, celery, apples and dates in a bowl. Mix the yoghurt with the mint and pour over the fruit. Serve garnished with chopped, roasted pistachio nuts.

Top: Pineapple, Orange and Sweetcorn Salad
Bottom: Cheese and Fruit Salad

MELON AND STRAWBERRY SALAD

Serves 6

1 large melon
350 g/12 oz strawberries, halved lengthways
juice of ½ lemon
2 tbsp sugar
sprig of mint
juice of 1 orange
100 ml/3½ fl oz dry sherry

Halve the melon, remove the seeds, scoop out and chop the flesh. Soak the strawberries in the lemon juice.

Boil the sugar and mint in a saucepan, with enough water to just cover, until a syrup forms. Remove the mint and stir in the orange juice and sherry.

Arrange the melon and strawberries in individual bowls and pour over the syrup. Garnish with mint. Alternatively, use small melons and arrange the strawberries in the scooped-out half shells.

ORANGE SALAD

Serves 4

5 oranges
2 large potatoes
1 beetroot
2 bananas
1 lettuce heart, shredded
8 tbsp mayonnaise
salt
freshly ground white pepper
2 tbsp finely chopped parsley

Cut open 4 of the oranges by making zigzag incisions into them. Scoop out the flesh. Cook the potatoes and beetroot, peel and finely slice. Slice the bananas, and chop the flesh of the remaining orange. Place all the ingredients in a bowl and stir in the mayonnaise. Season with a little salt. Fill each of the orange skins with the mixture and serve, on a bed of shredded lettuce, sprinkled with finely chopped parsley.

Below: Melon and Strawberry Salad
Right: Orange Salad

APRICOT AND MEDLAR SALAD

Serves 6

5 tbsp sugar
1 kg/2¼ lb apricots, peeled and stoned
1 kg/2¼ lb medlars, peeled and coved
100 ml/3½ fl oz port

Place 4 tablespoons of the sugar in a large saucepan and pour in just enough water to cover the base of the pan. Add the fruit and simmer for 10 minutes. Cut the fruit into attractive slices and arrange on a serving dish. Sprinkle with the remaining sugar, pour on the port and chill for several hours.

BANANA AND YOGHURT SALAD

Serves 6

1 kg/2¼ lb bananas, peeled and sliced
300 ml/10 fl oz yoghurt
150 g/5 oz pine nuts

Mix the bananas with the yoghurt in a bowl and chill for 1 hour.
Sprinkle with the pine nuts and serve.

MANDARIN SALAD IN BASIL SYRUP

Serves 6

12 mandarins, peeled
225 ml/8 fl oz water
60 g/2 oz sugar
2 sprigs basil, chopped

Chill the mandarins. Boil the water with the sugar and basil, until you achieve a light, not thick, syrup. Allow to cool and pour over the mandarins.
Substitute cinammon for the basil, if liked.

FRIED HORS D'OEUVRES

SPINACH, PINE NUT AND CURRENT PASTIES

Serves 4

Pastry:
300 g/10 oz flour
100 g/3¹/₂ oz butter, melted
1 sachet of dried yeast
1 tbsp oil
1-2 tbsp water

salt
oil for frying

Stuffing:
400 g/14 oz spinach
2 egg yolks
150 ml/5 fl oz single cream
30 g/1 oz pine nuts
100 g/3¹/₂ oz currants, blanched

Make the pastry dough by mixing together the flour, melted butter, yeast, oil, water and salt. Roll out the dough and cut into rounds with a cutter or a mug. Collect, roll and cut out any off-cuts.

Wash, cook, drain and chop the spinach. Add the egg yolks and cream and mix. Season well.

Fry the pine nuts and currants together. Add the spinach, mix well and heat through until the mixture binds together.

Divide the stuffing equally between the dough circles and fold each one over. Seal the edges by pressing down with a fork.

Fry for about 10 minutes in plenty of oil and serve.

MASHED POTATO AND MEAT CROQUETTES

Serves 6

1.5 kg/3¹/₄ lb potatoes
45 g/1¹/₂ oz flour
1 egg, beaten
2 tbsp finely chopped parsley
1 tbsp grated cheese
salt
freshly ground black pepper
¹/₂ tsp grated nutmeg

Cook the potatoes in boiling, salted water. Peel when cool and mash, adding the flour and then the egg, parsley and the grated cheese and season with salt, pepper and nutmeg.

Filling:
100 g/3¹/₂ oz lard or butter
1 onion, peeled and finely chopped
1 tomato, skinned, seeded and chopped
100 g/3¹/₂ oz minced veal
100 g/3¹/₂ oz raisins
1 hard-boiled egg, shelled and chopped
salt
freshly ground black pepper
1 tsp sugar

Melt the lard or butter in a frying-pan and fry the onion until lightly coloured. Add the tomato and veal and allow to fry for a few minutes before adding the raisins and

Top: Spinach, Pine Nut and Currant Pasties
Bottom: Mashed Potato and Meat Croquettes

chopped egg. Season with salt and pepper and the sugar. Stir well.

Dust your hands with flour to prevent sticking. Take a tablespoon of the potato mixture and flatten it in the palm of your hand. Put a teaspoon of the filling in the centre and seal it by closing your hand to form a ball.

Dust with flour and fry in a light oil.

TUNA CROQUETTES

Serves 4

60 g/2 oz butter
200 g/7 oz flour
225 ml/8 fl oz milk
2 medium cans tuna
salt
1/4 tsp grated nutmeg
120 g/4 oz dried breadcrumbs
150 ml/5 fl oz vegetable oil
1 egg

Melt the butter in a saucepan. Stir in 150 g/5 oz flour and gradually add the milk. Bring to the boil, stirring constantly, add the tuna and continue stirring until it breaks up. Season with a little salt and the grated nutmeg, and allow to cool. Reserve.

Beat the egg in a bowl and 1 tbsp of the remaining flour.

Form the tuna mixture into small balls of equal size. Dust with the remaining flour, coat in the egg mixture and roll in breadcrumbs.

In a frying-pan, heat the oil and fry the croquettes in batches over high heat, taking care not to spoil their shape or fry too many at once, as they will stick together. Drain on kitchen paper and serve.

BIENMESABE

Serves 6

2 kg/4 1/2 lb dogfish, huss or rock salmon
3 garlic cloves
1 tsp paprika
2 tsp fresh oregano
1 tsp cumin seeds
salt
100 ml/3 1/2 fl oz sherry vinegar
170 g/6 oz flour

Ask your fishmonger to clean the fish and cut it into small pieces. Pound the garlic in a mortar, adding the paprika, oregano, cumin seeds and a little salt. Add the sherry vinegar and mix with 750 ml/1 1/4 pints water. Arrange the fish in a shallow dish, pour over the garlic mixture, cover and marinate for 1 day. Remove, drain,

Top: Tuna Croquettes
Bottom: Bienmesabe

dredge in flour and fry in oil until golden on the outside and cooked through.

PRAWN FRIES

Serves 4

1 kg/2 1/4 lb fresh prawns
300 g/10 oz flour
1 tsp vinegar

pinch salt
1 egg white

Bring 1 litre/1¾ pints of salted water to the boil. Add the prawns and cook for 2-3 minutes. Drain, reserve the water, and allow to cool. Remove the prawn heads and small legs, taking care that they do not break open.

Prepare a dough with the flour, vinegar and salt, adding the reserved water, a little at a time, until a thick batter is achieved. Stiffly beat the egg white and fold in.

Take each prawn by the tip of its tail and coat it in the batter. Fry in plenty of very hot oil, drain on kitchen paper and serve.

PAVIA SOLDIERS

Serves 6

300 g/10 oz salt cod
juice of 1 lemon
150 g/5 oz flour
10 g/1/3 oz fresh yeast
2 tbsp oil
14 tbsp water
salt

Soak the salt cod in cold water for 24 hours, changing the water several times. Drain, cut into small pieces and place into a bowl with the lemon juice.

Place the flour in a mixing bowl. Make a well in the centre and add the yeast, oil, water and a little salt. Stir until it becomes dough, cover and leave to rise.

Coat the salt cod pieces in the dough and fry in very hot oil.

FRIED ASPARAGUS TIPS

Serves 4

1 medium can white asparagus tips
10 g/1/3 oz flour
2 eggs, beaten
oil for frying
salt

Drain the asparagus tips and dry thoroughly. Dust with the flour and coat in beaten egg. Fry immediately in hot oil. Season with salt and serve.

HAM AND CHICKEN CROQUETTES

Serves 6

3 cooked chicken breasts, boned, skinned and diced
100 g/3½ oz ham, diced
750 ml/1¼ pints milk
45 g/1½ oz butter
60 g/2 oz flour
salt
½ tsp grated nutmeg
oil for frying
2 eggs, beaten
150 g/5 oz dry breadcrumbs

Melt the butter in a saucepan, add the flour and cook until lightly coloured. Add the milk a little at a time, stirring constantly to keep it smooth. Stir in the ham and chicken and cook over very low heat for about 20 minutes, or until thickened, without stirring. Do not allow the mixture to burn. Season with a little salt and the nutmeg. Pour the mixture into a shallow dish, spreading it out to cool.

Pour into a frying-pan, enough oil to cover the base of the pan generously, and bring to a very high heat. Meanwhile, shape the croquettes with the help of a spoon, dust with flour, then coat with egg and breadcrumbs. Fry, drain and serve immediately.

CHEESE SANDWICHES

Serves 4

12 slices slightly stale bread
200 ml/7 fl oz milk
6 slices cheese, e.g. Mozzarella
1 egg, beaten
oil for frying

Sauce:
60 g/2 oz butter
60 g/2 oz flour
450 ml/15 fl oz milk
salt
freshly ground black pepper
¼ tsp grated nutmeg

Soak the bread slices briefly in the milk and pat dry. To make the sauce, heat the butter in a saucepan, stir in the flour and gradually add the milk. Simmer for 10 minutes. Remove from the heat and season with salt and pepper and stir in the nutmeg.

Spread some of the sauce on one side of each piece of bread and top with a slice of cheese. Use another slice to close the sandwich. Coat in beaten egg and fry in

plenty of very hot oil.

VEGETABLE PASTIES

Serves 4

Dough:
5 tbsp good quality oil
5 tbsp milk
flour (see below)
salt
1 egg, beaten

Filling:
30 g/1 oz butter
1 onion, peeled and finely chopped
450 g/1 lb spinach
60 g/2 oz flour
200 ml/7 fl oz milk
salt
freshly ground black pepper
¼ tsp nutmeg

:Place the milk in a mixing bowl with a pinch of salt. Stir in enough flour to make a firm dough. Allow to rest for at least 1 hour.

Make a white sauce from the butter, flour and milk. Boil the spinach in salted water, drain, squeeze dry and chop finely. Melt a little butter in a frying-pan, add the onion and, when it takes colour, the spinach. Add the sauce and season with salt, pepper and the nutmeg. Simmer until very thick.

Preheat the oven to 200° C/400° F, gas mark 6. Roll out the dough on a lightly floured board, fairly thinly. Cut out rounds with a pastry cutter and place a tablespoon of filling in the centre of each one. Fold over and seal by pressing a fork all around the edge.

Coat with beaten egg and arrange on a damp baking tray. Bake in the oven until they turn golden.

Top: Fried Asparagus Tips
Bottom: Cheese Sandwiches

FRIED SANDWICHES

Serves 4

1/2 loaf bread, sliced, crust removed
450 ml/15 fl oz milk
200 g/7 oz sliced ham, e.g. York
2 eggs, beaten
oil for frying

Cut each bread slice in half diagonally. Soak in the milk, then sandwich together with the ham. Coat in beaten egg and fry in very hot oil.

CHEESE FRITTERS

Serves 4

freshly ground black pepper
1/4 tsp grated nutmeg
75 g/2 1/2 oz flour
2 eggs
1 level tsp fresh yeast
60 g/2 oz mature cheese, grated
oil for frying

Heat the milk, butter, salt, pepper and nutmeg in a saucepan. Bring to the boil and immediately remove from the heat. Add the flour all at once and stir vigorously with a wooden spoon until the dough leaves the sides of the pan. Allow to

cool a little.

While still warm, stir in the eggs, one at a time. Add the yeast and the grated cheese and allow to rest.

Pipe the mixture, cutting it to make short, fairly thick fingers, into a frying-pan of very hot oil. Fry until golden, remove, drain on kitchen paper and serve warm.

Left: Fried Sandwiches
Below: Cheese Fritters

HAM AND CHEESE BALLS

Serves 4

6 egg whites
150 g/5 oz Gruyère cheese, grated
75 g/2½ oz ham, finely chopped
4 tbsp breadcrumbs
2 eggs, beaten
salt
freshly ground black pepper
oil for frying

Beat the egg whites in a bowl until they form peaks. Fold in the cheese, finely chopped ham and a little salt and pepper to form a stiff mixture. Shape into little balls. Roll in breadcrumbs, coat with beaten egg and roll in breadcrumbs again. Fry in very hot oil.

COD FRITTERS

Serves 4

225 g/8 oz cod
450 g/1 lb potatoes
2 eggs, beaten
oil for frying

Poach the cod in lightly salted water for 12-15 minutes. Drain and flake the fish.

Meanwhile boil the potatoes in lightly salted water. Allow to cool, peel and mash. Add the eggs and a little oil and stir until smooth. Add the fish. Shape the mixture into little balls and fry in plenty of hot oil.

EGG HORS D'OEUVRES

EGGS WITH SPINACH IN A SHELL

Serves 4

450 g/1 lb spinach
60 g/2 oz butter
2 tbsp flour
90 ml/3 fl oz milk
4 eggs, beaten
60 g/2 oz cheese, grated
salt
freshly ground black pepper
1/4 tsp grated nutmeg

Cook the spinach for 10 minutes in boiling, salted water. Drain, squeeze dry and chop finely. Sauté in a pan in a little butter.

In a saucepan, heat most of the remaining butter, stir in the flour and cook until lightly coloured. Gradually add the milk, then the eggs and half the cheese. Season with salt, pepper and nutmeg. Remove from heat when thickened.

Preheat the oven to 220° C/425° F, gas mark 7. Prepare 4 scallop shells and press a quarter of the spinach into each. Top with the egg mixture and sprinkle with the remaining cheese. Melt the remaining butter and pour over. Bake in the oven until golden.

EGGS IN TOMATO

Serves 6

6 uniformly sized tomatoes
salt
fresh ground black pepper
6 tbsp finely chopped ham
6 eggs
butter
225 g/8 oz peas
225 g/8 oz carrots, peeled and finely sliced

Preheat the oven to 220° C/425° F, gas mark 7. Slice the tops off the tomatoes and scoop out the flesh. Season with salt and pepper. Add a tablespoon of the ham and break an egg into each one. Top with a little butter. Place on a baking tray and cook in the oven for 10 minutes.

Boil the peas and carrots separately in salted water. Drain and sauté in some butter and reserve.

Arrange the tomatoes on a dish, garnish with the peas and carrots, and triangles of fried bread, if liked.

SALT COD OMELETTES

Serves 6

450 g/1 lb salt cod
2 onions, peeled and finely chopped
2 tbsp butter
2 garlic cloves, peeled and finely chopped
2 eggs, beaten

Soak the salt cod pieces for 24 hours, changing the cold water at least 3 times. Squeeze dry, skin, bone and shred the fish.

Sauté the chopped onions in the butter until lightly coloured. Add the garlic. Stir in the salt cod and cook, stirring, for about 10 minutes. Add the eggs to make the omelette.

As soon as it is cooked, remove and cut into small pieces and serve on cocktail sticks. Alternatively, serve whole, garnished with strips of pepper, if liked.

CAVIAR EGGS

Serves 4

2 shallots, peeled and finely chopped
60ml/2 fl oz olive oil
2 tsp white wine vinegar
salt
freshly ground black pepper
4 hard-boiled eggs, shelled
1 small jar caviar or lumpfish roe
2 tomatoes, sliced
bunch of watercress

Combine the shallots with the oil, vinegar, salt and pepper. Halve the eggs, and remove the yolks and mash into the shallot mixture. Stir in the caviar or lumpfish roe. Using the egg whites as boats for the mixture, divide it evenly between them. Serve on the tomato slices and garnish with the watercress.

BAKED EGGS

Serves 4

45 g/11/2 oz butter
200 g/7 oz Emmenthal cheese, grated
4 eggs
45 ml/11/2 fl oz cream
salt
1/4 tsp grated nutmeg

Preheat the oven to 180° C/350° F, gas mark 4. Butter 4 individual cocottes. Divide 60 g/2 oz of the cheese between them and break in the eggs, taking care not to break the yolks. Pour on the cream, add the remaining cheese, season with salt and nutmeg, and top off with a knob of butter. Bake in the oven for 15-20 minutes.

Top: Eggs with Spinach in a Shell
Bottom: Salt Cod Omelettes

EGG CROQUETTES

Serves 4

30 g/1 oz butter
6 tbsp flour
450 ml/15 fl oz milk
4 hard-boiled eggs, shelled and finely chopped
1/2 tsp grated nutmeg
salt
freshly ground black pepper
1 egg, beaten
150 g/5 oz dry breadcrumbs
oil for frying

Melt the butter in a saucepan, add 4 tablespoons of flour and allow to cook without colouring. Add the milk, a little at a time, stirring constantly to keep the sauce smooth. Cook for 8 minutes, then add the chopped eggs and nutmeg and season with salt and pepper. Pour on to a dish and allow to cool. Make the croquettes with a little of the mixture at a time. Dust with the remaining flour, coat with beaten egg and then breadcrumbs. Fry in very hot oil.

EGG AND TOMATO TOADSTOOLS

Serves 6

mayonnaise
6 hard-boiled eggs, shelled
3 small tomatoes, halved
1 lettuce, shredded

Spread some thick mayonnaise on to a small serving dish. Cut the bottoms off the eggs and stand them up in the dish. Place the tomato halves on top of the eggs to form the toadstool caps and garnish with the shredded lettuce.

STUFFED EGGS

Serves 4

4 hard-boiled eggs, shelled
60 g/2 oz ham, e.g. Serrano, finely diced
1 small can tuna, crumbled
450 g/1 lb whole spinach leaves, blanched
4 tbsp light mayonnaise

Cut the eggs in half. Remove the yolks and reserve, taking care not to damage the whites.

Mash 2 of the yolks and combine with the ham and tuna to make a paste. Use to fill the egg whites.

Arrange a bed of blanched spinach leaves in a serving dish. Place the eggs on top, dress with a light mayonnaise, and sieve over the remaining yolks. Garnish with some olives, if liked.

Top: Egg and Tomato Toadstools
Bottom: Stuffed Eggs

VEGETABLE HORS D'OEUVRES

ITALIAN POTATOES

Serves 4

1 kg/2¹/₄ lb medium potatoes, peeled
300 g/10 oz butter, melted
salt
2 tsp rosemary leaves

Preheat the oven to 220° C/425° F, gas mark 7. Cut each potato into 4 even pieces and place in a baking tin. Pour over the melted butter, season with salt and bake in the oven for about 1 hour, basting occasionally. Sprinkle with rosemary 30 minutes before the end of cooking time.

STUFFED TOMATOES

Serves 4

4 medium tomatoes
1 onion, peeled and finely chopped
30 g/1 oz butter
15 g/¹/₂ oz sliced bread
100 ml/3¹/₂ fl oz milk
1 egg, beaten
100 g/3¹/₂ oz cheese, grated
1 tsp finely chopped parsley
¹/₂ tsp grated nutmeg
salt
freshly ground black pepper

Slice the top off each tomato, scoop out the insides and stand, upside down, on a wire rack to drain. Fry the onion in half the butter in a frying-pan until lightly coloured. Remove from the heat. Soak the bread in the milk, squeeze dry and add to the pan. Add the egg, half the cheese, the parsley and nutmeg and season with salt and pepper. Mix well and stuff the tomatoes with this mixture. Melt the remaining butter and pour over the tomatoes. Sprinkle with the remaining cheese and place under the grill to brown for a few minutes.

AUBERGINES WITH SAUSAGE

Serves 4

3 aubergines
salt
3 tomatoes, sliced
250 g/9 oz green peppers, seeded and sliced
250 g/9 oz saveloy sausages, diced

Cut the aubergines in half lengthways, sprinkle with salt and leave to dégorge for 30 minutes. Rinse off all the moisture, remove the seeds and dry with paper towels. Fry the tomatoes, peppers and aubergine halves together for 30 minutes. In a separate pan, fry the diced sausages for 5 minutes, add the aubergine mixture and cook for 10 minutes. Serve.

Top: Italian Potatoes
Bottom: Stuffed Tomatoes

MUSHROOMS AU GRATIN

Serves 4

100 g/3½ oz butter
450 g/1 lb button mushrooms, trimmed
juice of 1 lemon
1 onion, peeled and finely chopped
salt
1 tbsp flour
200 ml/7 fl oz milk
75 ml/2½ fl oz cream
1 egg yolk
30 g/1 oz cheese, grated

Melt half the butter in a large saucepan.
Add the mushrooms, lemon juice, onion
and a little salt. Cover and cook over low
heat for 20 minutes.
    Make a Béchamel sauce by cooking the
flour in all but 15 g/½ oz of the remaining
butter, adding the milk gradually and stir
constantly to keep it smooth. Cook for 8
minutes, remove from the heat and add
the cream.
Return to the heat and cook for a few
more minutes, stirring. Remove, add the
egg yolk and season with salt.
    Drain the mushrooms thoroughly, place
in an ovenproof dish and pour over the
sauce. Sprinkle with the grated cheese.
Melt the remaining butter and pour over.
Place under the grill to brown for a few
minutes.

CELERY AND CHEESE

Serves 4

1 head celery
300 g/10 oz blue cheese

Clean and wash the celery, discarding the
leaves. Cut into 4 cm/1½ inch pieces.
Melt the cheese and serve it in a dish as a
dip for the celery sticks.

MUSHROOMS STUFFED WITH PRAWNS

Serves 4

300 g/10 oz cooked prawns
1 tbsp chopped parsley
1 garlic clove
oil for frying
1 kg/2¼ lb button mushrooms, stalks removed
salt
juice of 1 lemon (optional)

Shell the prawns and chop finely. Mince the parsley and garlic together and mix with the prawns.

Heat a little oil in a large frying-pan. Arrange the mushrooms in the pan, cup side up, then stuff with the prawn mixture. Cook over a high heat for a few minutes until heated through. Remove and season with salt and lemon juice, if liked.

ALIOLI POTATOES

Serves 4

4 potatoes
2 garlic cloves
salt
300 ml/10 fl oz mayonnaise

Boil the potatoes in plenty of salted water until tender. Drain, cool and peel. Slice them and arrange on a serving dish.

Pound the garlic with some salt and add these to the mayonnaise, stirring well to blend. Pour over the potatoes and serve.

Left: Mushrooms Au Gratin
Below: Alioli Potatoes

MEAT HORS D'OEUVRES

COLD MEAT LOAF

Serves 4

6 eggs
100 ml/3¹/₂ fl oz milk
60 g/2 oz butter, melted
pinch salt
¹/₂ oz butter for greasing
8 slices bread, crusts removed
500 g/1 lb 2 oz cooked ham
8 slices cheese

Beat together the eggs, milk, melted butter
and salt.

Preheat the oven to 180° C/350° F, gas
mark 4. Butter a non-stick loaf tin. Line
the bottom with bread and a generous
layer of the beaten egg mixture. Add a
layer of ham, then cheese, then put more
bread over this, and coat again with the
egg mixture. Continue layering until the
mould is full, finishing with a layer of egg.
Make incisions in the loaf with a knife so
that the liquid penetrates to the bottom.

Place in a bain-marie and cook in the
oven for 1¹/₂ hours. Allow to cool, then
turn on to a serving dish and serve sliced.

VITELLO TONNATO

Serves 6

1 small can tuna
2 tbsp capers
3 anchovies
300 ml/10 fl oz thin mayonnaise
1 kg/2¹/₄ lb cooked veal, sliced

Mash together the tuna, capers and
anchovies. Beat into the mayonnaise.
Arrange the veal slices in a serving dish
and pour over the tuna sauce.Garnish with
gherkins, extra capers or lemon slices, if
liked.

SOUSED CHICKEN BREASTS

Serves 4

4 chicken breasts
450 ml/15 fl oz water
6 tbsp olive oil
225 ml/8 fl oz sherry vinegar
2 onions, peeled and chopped

2 leeks, chopped
4 carrots, peeled and chopped
2 garlic cloves, chopped
1 tsp thyme
1 bayleaf
1 tsp green peppercorns
salt

Place the chicken breasts in a saucepan and
pour over the water, oil and vinegar. Add
the remaining ingredients, cover and
simmer for 1 hour.

Remove the chicken breasts, skin and
bone them, then arrange on a dish and
serve.

CHICKEN QUICHE

Serves 6

Pastry:
75 g/2¹/₂ oz butter
150 g/5 oz flour
1 egg, beaten
1 tbsp milk
salt

Filling:
45 g/1¹/₂ oz butter
150 g/5 oz cooked chicken, finely chopped
60 g/2 oz ham, finely chopped
1 tbsp flour
75 ml/2¹/₂ fl oz milk
30 ml/1 fl oz sherry
1 tbsp chopped parsley
salt
freshly ground black pepper
2 egg yolks, beaten

To make the pastry, rub the butter into
the flour. Add the egg, milk and salt.
Knead the dough until soft but not too
elastic. Allow to rest for 20 minutes.

To make the filling, melt the butter in a
saucepan. Add the chicken and cook for 2
minutes. Add the ham and stir for a few
more minutes. Stir in the flour, then the
milk, sherry and chopped parsley. Simmer
for 10 minutes, season and stir in the egg
yolks. Reserve.

Preheat the oven to 180° C/350° F, gas
mark 4. Roll out the pastry and use to line
1 medium-sized flan tin or 6 individual
ones. Pour in the filling and bake in the
oven for about 20 minutes. Remove and
allow to cool a little before serving.

CHICKEN FRITTERS

Serves 6

200 ml/7 fl oz water
60 g/2 oz butter
pinch salt
freshly ground black pepper
100 g/3¹/₂ oz flour
3 large eggs, beaten
100 g/3¹/₂ oz roast chicken, finely chopped
60 g/2 oz ham, finely chopped
30 g/1 oz cheese, grated
oil for deep-frying

Bring the water, butter and salt to the boil.
Pour in all the flour at once, stir
vigorously until the mixture forms a ball.
Remove from the heat when it no longer
sticks to the sides of the pan. Turn out and
allow to cool slightly.

While still warm, add the beaten eggs, a
little at a time, blending thoroughly.

Add the chicken, ham and cheese to the
mixture and keep warm.

Heat the oil in a deep-fryer to 190°
C/375° F or until a cube of stale bread
turns golden in 30 seconds. Make the
fritters by scooping out a little of the
mixture with 2 teaspoons (they will swell
in size as they cook). Fry in batches,
allowing room for swelling. Serve very hot
on a napkin.

Top: Chicken Quiche
Bottom: Chicken Fritters

MIXED MEAT HORS D'OEUVRES

LIVER AND BACON

Serves 4

150 g/5 oz liver, finely chopped
150 g/5 oz bacon, finely chopped
150 ml/5 fl oz single cream
1/2 onion, peeled and finely chopped
1 tbsp chopped parsley
salt
freshly ground black pepper
4 slices wholemeal bread

Fry the liver and bacon together for about 5 minutes, stirring, until the liver is cooked through but not hard. Stir in enough single cream to moisten, simmer until reduced. Add the onion and parsley, season with salt and pepper and serve spread on the bread slices.

BARCELONA BITES

Serves 4

450 g/1 lb mixed offal (liver, kidneys, sweetbread etc), finely chopped
1 tbsp finely chopped onion
2 garlic cloves, finely chopped

Fry all the ingredients together in some oil, stirring, for 10-15 minutes. Serve on small pieces of bread or in individual pots.

BLACK PUDDING IN TOMATO SAUCE

Serves 4

8 thin slices bread, crusts removed
2 black puddings, sliced
oil for frying
150 ml/5 fl oz fresh tomato sauce, heated

Cut the bread slices into small pieces, each large enough fit one slice of black pudding. Fry the black pudding in a little oil over a low heat. Arrange on the pieces of bread and garnish with hot tomato sauce.

LAMB'S SWEETBREADS

Serves 2

225 g/8 oz sweetbreads
pinch salt
water for poaching
60 g/2 oz flour
2 eggs, beaten
oil for frying

Poach the sweetbreads in salted water for 25 minutes. Allow to cool, dust with the flour, coat with the egg and fry in oil. Serve hot.

LIVER WITH OREGANO

Serves 4

8 slices bread, crusts removed
2 tbsp oil
500 g/1 lb 2 oz lamb's liver, chopped
2 tsp oregano
juice of 1 lemon
salt
freshly ground black pepper
1 tbsp finely chopped parsley

Cut the bread into small pieces. Heat the oil in a frying-pan and cook the liver in for 2 minutes. Add the oregano and lemon juice, season with salt and pepper, turn down the heat and simmer for 10 minutes. Sprinkle with the parsley and serve on the bread.

KIDNEY BROCHETTES

Serves 4

450 g/1 lb kidneys, skinned
4 tbsp olive oil
salt

Halve the kidneys and remove the white core. Thread on to skewers, brush with oil and season with salt. Cook on a barbecue or hot griddle and serve on the skewers.

LAMB'S LIVER WITH PEPPERS

Serves 2

225 g/8 oz lamb's liver, sliced
1 tbsp chopped parsley
1 garlic clove, chopped
1/2 tsp salt
1 egg, beaten
breadcrumbs
oil for frying
450 g/1 lb red peppers

Sprinkle the liver with the parsley, garlic and salt and allow to soak for a few minutes. Coat the slices with beaten egg and breadcrumbs. Heat 6 tbsp oil in a frying-pan and fry the meat on a moderate heat. Roast the peppers over a flame until the skin turns black, skin, slice and reserve any juices. Fry the pepper slices and add to the liver. Add the juices and bring to the boil. Serve hot.

LIVER AND TOMATO

Serves 6

700 g/1 1/2 lb lamb's liver, diced
salt
5 tbsp olive oil
1 onion, peeled and sliced
1 kg/2 1/4 lb tomatoes, skinned, seeded and diced

Season the liver with salt and fry in 4 tbsp oil, together with the onion. In a separate pan, fry the tomatoes in the remaining oil. Season with salt, and when the liquid has completely reduced, add to the liver and continue to fry for a further 10 minutes, until the juices evaporate, leaving only the oil. Serve on a large dish.

Top: Liver with Oregano
Bottom: Kidney Brochettes

SEAFOOD HORS D'OEUVRES

ANCHOVIES IN BATTER

Serves 6

1 kg/2¼ lb small, fresh anchovies
salt
100 g/3½ oz flour
2 eggs, beaten
oil for frying
2 lemons, cut in wedges

Remove the backbones from the anchovies but leave their tails on. Open them out and season with salt, dust with flour, coat with beaten egg and fry in hot oil. Drain and serve hot or cold, accompanied by lemon wedges.

HAKE WITH GARLIC

Serves 6

1 kg/2¼ lb hake or cod fillets, skinned
salt
100 g/3½ oz flour
2 eggs, beaten
2 garlic cloves, chopped
75 ml/2½ oz oil
1 lettuce, shredded
4 lemons, cut in wedges

Cut the fish fillets into bite-sized pieces, discarding any bones. Season with salt and dust with flour, shaking off any excess. Coat with beaten egg and leave to drain.

Sauté the garlic in the oil in a large pan and remove with a spatula just as it takes colour. Turn down the heat and gently fry the fish pieces, a few at a time, so that they do not stick. Do not overcook, as it will lose its special flavour and texture. The fish is ready as soon as it becomes firm.

Drain on kitchen paper and serve hot on a bed of shredded lettuce, garnished with lemon wedges.

FROG'S LEGS

Serves 4

12 pairs frogs' legs
salt
freshly ground black pepper
juice of 1 lemon
100 g/3½ oz flour
2 eggs, beaten
oil for frying

Trim the frogs' legs and marinate for 2 hours in salt, pepper and lemon juice. Dust with flour, coat in beaten egg and fry in hot oil.

SEA BREAM MOULDS

Serves 6

1 kg/2¼ lb sea bream or bass
1 litre/1¾ pints fish stock
5 eggs, beaten
salt
freshly ground black pepper
2 tbsp butter
6 tbsp dried breadcrumbs
1 can pimentos, drained and cut into strips

Simmer the fish in the stock for 20 minutes or until the flesh comes away easily from the bone. Drain, then flake the flesh.

Stir the flaked fish into the beaten eggs. Season with salt and pepper and mix well. Butter 6 individual moulds and sprinkle with breadcrumbs. Pour in the fish mixture to come three-quarters of the way up the sides, and chill for at least 30 minutes.

Meanwhile, preheat the oven to 180° F/350° F, gas mark 4. Place the moulds in a bain-marie and cook in the oven at for about 30 minutes, covering with foil after 15 minutes, to prevent drying out.

Turn out on to a dish and garnish with pimento strips.

WHITEBAIT

Serves 4

1 kg/2¼ lb whitebait
300 g/10 oz flour
oil for frying
salt
2 lemons cut in wedges

Wash the whitebait thoroughly and dry. Dredge in the flour. Fry them in the oil, on not too high a heat. Serve sprinkled with salt in warmed bowls, accompanied by wedges of lemon.

HAKE FILLETS IN CURRY MAYONNAISE

Serves 4

1 kg/2¼ lb hake fillets, skinned
salt
30 g/1 oz butter
juice of 1 lemon
1 tsp curry paste
150 ml/5 fl oz mayonnaise
8 thin slices of bread

Preheat the oven to 180° C/350° F, gas mark 4. Slice the hake into small pieces and season with salt. Butter a baking dish, arrange the hake in it, squeeze over some lemon juice and bake in the oven for about 10 minutes. Allow to cool completely. Stir the curry paste into the mayonnaise and use to dress the fish. Serve on the bread.

Top: Frogs' Legs
Bottom: Hake Fillets in Curry Mayonnaise

TXANGURRO

Serves 6

1 onion, roughly chopped
1 leek, roughly chopped
2 carrots, roughly chopped
1 garlic clove, chopped
1 crab
2 tbsp olive oil
100 ml/3½ fl oz sherry or brandy
150 ml/5 fl oz fresh tomato sauce
100 ml/3½ fl oz double cream
2 tbsp breadcrumbs
2 tbsp chopped parsley (optional)

Txangurro is Basque for both crab and this way of preparing it.

Bring a large pan of water to the boil, add the onion, leek, carrots and garlic. Add the crab after a few moments and allow to cook for about 25 minutes, depending on the size and weight. Drain and allow to cool. Reserve the vegetables.

Split open the crab with a knife. Use the top shell as a serving dish. Scoop out the brown meat and extract as much white meat as possible from the claws. Discard the gills and intestines.

Chop the reserved vegetables and heat through in a frying-pan with the oil. Add all the crab meat and juices. Stir and add the sherry or brandy and tomato sauce. Gradually stir in the cream, so the mixture thickens slightly.

Preheat the oven to 220° C/425° F, gas mark 7. Pour the crab mixture into the crab shell, add a knob of butter and place in the oven to brown for about 5 minutes.

Garnish with breadcrumbs and chopped parsley, if liked.

Txangurro

CANAPÉS

ANCHOVY CANAPÉS

Serves 4

6 slices bread
1 can anchovies
60 g/2 oz butter

1 gherkin, sliced
1 hard-boiled egg, shelled and chopped

Toast the bread and cut into squares. Reserve a few anchovies and mash the remainder with the butter to form a paste. Spread on the toast, garnish with the reserved anchovies, cut into strips, sliced gherkin and chopped egg.

ASPARAGUS AND WALNUT CANAPÉS

Serves 4

1 can asparagus tips
150 g/5 oz butter
4 slices bread
1 egg yolk, beaten
squeeze of lemon juice
1 tbsp single cream
60 g/2 oz walnuts, chopped
salt
freshly ground black pepper

Heat the can of asparagus in a bain-marie. Spread the bread slices with half the butter and toast under the grill. Gently heat the egg yolk with the lemon juice in a small pan, stirring. Add the remaining butter in small pieces, allowing each to melt before adding the next. Remove from the heat, and, still stirring, add the cream, chopped walnuts, salt and pepper. Drain the asparagus, arrange on the toast and dress with the sauce. Serve immediately.

GHERKIN AND TOMATO CANAPÉS

Serves 4

4 tsp mayonnaise
4 slices of white bread
2 tomatoes, thinly sliced
salt
freshly ground black pepper
2 small onions, thinly sliced
4 gherkins, thinly sliced lengthways

Toast the bread and spread with the mayonnaise. Add the tomato and season. Top with thinly sliced onion and cucumber. Serve.

Left Top: Asparagus and Walnut Canapés
Left Bottom: Anchovy Canapés
Right: Egg Canapé surrounded by Gherkin and Tomato Canapés

EGG CANAPÉS

Serves

4 thick slices of bread
2 tbsp butter
4 slices ham

2 hard-boiled eggs, shelled and halved
1 egg yolk
300 ml/10 fl oz Béchamel sauce
60 g/2 oz Parmesan cheese, grated
freshly ground black pepper

Toast the bread and butter it. On each

slice, place a slice of ham, and half a hard-boiled egg, face down. Preheat the grill to a medium heat. Stir the egg yolk into the Béchamel sauce and pour over the bread slices. Sprinkle with grated Parmesan cheese and pepper to taste. Brown under the grill. Serve immediately.

PRAWN CANAPÉS

Serves 4

450 g/1 lb cooked prawns
1 tbsp lemon juice
1 small can pimentos, chopped
2 tbsp chopped onion
Tabasco
4 tbsp mayonnaise

Peel and clean the prawns thoroughly.
Heat gently in a saucepan with a little
water, drain and chop. Place in a bowl and
mash in the lemon juice, pimentos, onion,
Tabasco and mayonnaise. Spread on bread
slices or fill vol-au-vents.

CHICKEN VOL-AU-VENTS

Serves 4

1 onion, finely chopped
60 g/2 oz butter
2 cooked chicken breasts, chopped
100 ml/3½ fl oz white wine
75 g/2½ oz flour
100 ml/3½ fl oz milk
100 ml/3½ fl oz stock
1 hard-boiled egg, shelled and finely chopped
salt
freshly ground black pepper
½ tsp grated nutmeg
8 vol-au-vent cases

Sauté the onion in the butter, until lightly
coloured. Add the chicken, then stir in the
wine and simmer until reduced. Stir in the
flour, cook for a few minutes, then add
the milk and stock. Cook until reduced to
a thick sauce. Remove from the heat, add
the chopped egg and season with salt,
pepper and nutmeg. Meanwhile, preheat
the oven to 180° C/350° F, gas mark 4.
Fill the vol-au-vents with the mixture and
warm through in the oven.

SKATE LIVER CANAPÉS

Serves 6

2 skate livers
300 ml/10 fl oz court bouillon
bouquet garni
6 thick slices wholemeal bread
45 g/1½ oz butter
juice of 1 lemon

Skate is an excellent fish, best served with black butter or garlic sauce. The livers are rarely available in this country but can be replaced with fresh cod's roe.

Simmer the livers in the court bouillon with the bouquet garni. Allow to cool. Divide the liver between the bread slices. Melt the butter in a pan and pour over the liver. Sprinkle with lemon juice and serve.

MIDNIGHT FEAST

Serves 6

100 g/3½ oz butter
100 g/3½ oz flour
450 ml/¾ pint milk, warmed
100 g/3½ oz liver pâté
60 g/2 oz cheese, grated
salt
12 round bread rolls

Melt half the butter in a saucepan, stir in the flour and cook for 2 minutes. Gradually stir in the warm milk and cook, stirring, for 8 minutes. Add the pâté, a tablespoon of the cheese and a little salt.

Preheat the oven to 220° C/425° F, gas mark 7. Cut the bread rolls in half, discard some of the crumb carefully, fill with the pâté mixture, cover and allow to cool.

Place on a baking tray. Melt the remaining butter and pour over. Sprinkle on the remaining cheese and cook in the oven for 5–10 minutes, until brown.

Left: Chicken Vol-au-Vents
Below: Skate Liver Canapés

INDEX